I0470613

Your First Online Store

A Beginners Guide:
Starting a Drop Shipping Business

George N Astras

DEDICATION

I want to dedicate this book to my two lovely daughter. You are a constant reminder that life is great.

CONTENTS

ACKNOWLEDGMENTS

I want to thank my wife Kelly for the constant support, and motivation in writing this book. I also want to thank Amazon for providing me the opportunity to write, and self-publish.

1 REALITY CHECK

As you may have noticed that the internet has exploded, and has made many people rich. The people making money right now aren't smarter, or better then you. They just have a successful company, and the truth is that you can also have a successful company.

This book is a guide to get your online business started. Everything that you need to get started is covered. If you follow the book correctly, you will not only have one successful site, but many more to follow. It reveals the basics to get you started.

There are certain things you need to understand, before you get started. I want to take the time to debunk many theories that other books have created. Many authors want you to buy their book, and all start with building up the reader. They promise, that you will be rich beyond your wildest dreams.

These type of books are great for motivation, however they lack the manual to accomplish the wealth. I found a similar passage in three different books. I am not quoting, but this is along those lines. *Starting an online site is easy, there are many companies out there that will help you get started. Think of the wealth you will be earning.* Great, I now know that I can try to figure out how to start a webpage. They give a statistical number of how many people start an online business each day. Statistical numbers, won't help you ascertain wealth.

I want to make a comparison. Let's say you went to a weight loss convention. You walk around, looking for a fool proof way to lose weight. You stumble upon two tables, the first table has a banner, that states Lose Weight Safely. The second table has a banner that states, Lose Weight Fast.

Although you feel inclined to visit the first table, you cannot resist and visit the second table. The person at the second table tells you, buy his pills, and drink his shakes. The best part is you never have to exercise. In 30 days, you would have lost 80 pounds. At the first table, the person tries to tells you, he has a workout out program, and a healthy diet plan. If you exercise 30 minutes a day, and eat right you can lose up to 8 pounds a month.

The sad truth is that the second table would have more people buying into the pills, and shakes. The more desperate the person is, the more willing they will be to sign up with table #2. Less effort, with better results is the most convincing method. The health risks will be ignored, and there is no thought of long term.

You have to put effort, and be patient. It will take time, to build up to a steady income. It doesn't happen overnight. You have to be the type of person that is willing to exercise hard, and put effort into achieving your goal.

I am going to show you, how to start a successful drop shipping website. You will be selling merchandise that you didn't have to buy, until you sell the item. This means that you don't need to keep inventory.

All this will be explained in detail in later chapters. To simplify the concept, you will create a website, and upload products that a drop shipping supplier has available. You will sell their products for a profit. Each time you make a sale, you place an order with your supplier, and they will ship directly to your customer. The difference in price is your profit.

The type of income from starting such a site isn't going to be tremendous. However once you are established it will be a steady flow, with low overhead. The longer you are around the more people will know about your store. If you decide to expand, you can have multiple sources of steady flow.

With a well place strategy, you will be able to draw customers to your site, and generate sales. I will be suggesting products, and a few companies. I do not make any money or profit from any of the suggestions. Through my experience, I can recommend a hosting company for your site, which credit card processing company, which software to use as a shopping cart.

In an effort to avoid any lawsuits, I can't tell which companies to stay away from. Instead I will be providing you with warnings. One such warning, will be to never pay a monthly fee to a drop shipper. So you found one that charges a monthly fee, that is the company to stay away from.

There are certain things that current successful running sites have, that you will not have when you first start. This is the part that I want to stress again, do not rush the process. If you haven't made your first sale, it isn't wise to print catalogs. Do not hire someone to answer phones, or rent a warehouse. You don't need an 800 number just yet. When your business grows, then you can expand and start spending money. One thing to keep in mind is that Sears started as a catalog.

I want to go over the type of person that can run a business. It is something that is overlooked, and you need to be aware of it. You have to have a positive attitude. If you have failed before, then your new attitude has to be that you truly believe you can do this. I will touch on each subject briefly, even though entire chapters can be dedicated to each topic. I want to move through this quickly, and get you started.

Organization

You have to be organized, and keep records. If you are sloppy, and live in disorder, you need to change that right now. You don't have to file things alphabetically, but you do need to be able to find things. If you're not going to keep neat files, then keep them anyway you can. Clear out a desk draw, or use shoe boxes. Label one box expenses, and the other profits. Every time you buy something business related, drop the receipt in the box. Although your drop shipper will probably have electronic receipts print them anyway. Print your invoices, and keep everything. Print your Google, and Bing expenses, print everything. An expense can easily be forgotten, when you have to log in somewhere, and look for it.

Create a method to remind yourself of to do lists. A note book or piece of paper is the best and cheapest method. Leave it somewhere visible, where you will see it every day. Write all your tasks down. If you told a customer you will call him back on Monday, write that down. When the task is done cross it out. If you get a cut off notice for the internet bill, write it down so you won't forget it. Write down all your tasks. This might seem irrelevant in the beginning. You can easily remember the few tasks at hand. However you are training yourself, for a long lasting business. Being organized is very important, and shouldn't be ignored. Even if your website is a hobby, don't treat it as such.

Adaptability

One thing is certain in every business. Trends change, and so does the style of doing business. You have to be able to accept that your brilliant idea, might of stopped working. You have to be willing to change your methods, and keep up with your competition. I am reminded of suppliers, that refused to create an online store, and stuck to their printed yearly catalog. They all would insist that they have been in business for thirty plus years. I watched their new competition that started five years ago surpass them.

Another thing in the business world, is to have the ability to bounce back. Things will not always go according to plan. You can't dwell on failures for days, and start thinking of closing. If you get several fraudulent orders, it's real easy to get depressed over the money you lost. You have to survive the setback, and change how you do business. Your supplier goes out of business. Instead of looking for a new supplier, it might be time for a new fresher item.

Let's take a very quick look at Amazon.com. The site is up and running since 1995. It started out by selling just books. Since that time the company has adapted, and survived the .com boom. If you visit the website today, you will see it is now much more than a bookstore. It operates other websites, and is has spurred into many other companies. As the company grew, so did its ability to adapt.

Positive Attitude

You have to be mentally strong, to strive big. The setbacks that you have experienced in your life, should be put into your past. They should be a memory. They can't be in your future. You have to be, and believe that you are the best, and will be successful.

I am reminded of an interviewers style. He was a high ranking Officer in charge of the Detective unit, and was interviewing Police Officers that wanted to join his unit. After reviewing the applicants, he set up one interview day. He had seven possible, candidates come to his office, and had them wait in the hallway. He called in the first officer, into his office. He stated to the Officer, there are six people sitting out there for this position. He asked the Officer to tell him why he is better than all of them.

I want you to imagine yourself, in this position. Picture yourself in your current, or past job. How would you answer this question? You are being asked to compare yourself to your co-workers. Aren't they your friends? Do you want to make yourself look better than them? If this how your thought process is going, WRONG ATTITUDE. The people in the hallway are your competition.

The Officer in this scenario responded humbly, that he isn't better. That one of the Officers waiting, is more experienced, and is very active. Before the officer can finish, the office door was opened, and he was jested to walk towards it. On his way out he was told to tell the more experienced officer to come in.

The interviewer only wants winning attitudes. He only wants the best Police Officers to work for him. This attitude may seem conceded. However it takes this type of attitude, to be successful. He felt that if you lack the positive attitude about yourself, then you lacked the motivation to be successful in his unit.

Time Management

A key aspect of being your own boss, is that you control your day. If you follow the steps correctly you will only be spending a few hours a week to keep the site running profitably. The thing to be careful is when your days become overloaded, or you are taking on too many projects. It's fine, to have a full time job, and be raising children. The problem comes into play, when you join too many clubs, or start several projects at the same time. You will find yourself, never finishing anything.

It's important that you complete your website project, before you take on any other projects. You need to dedicate the time each day. You will use this time to enter new orders, update your inventory, configure your advertising, and other tasks on your to do list. You have to allocate this time. If you have a smart phone, you can do most of this on your lunch break. The more time you are able to allocate, the better for the business.

Money Management

Let's imagine you saw the wealthy Donald Trump in the supermarket, and you observed him using coupons. What would your reaction be? It's a funny scenario, but the truth is that many wealthy Americans have this type of discipline. They might not be using coupons, but they will not spend a penny more if they don't have to.

Train yourself now to nip spending, and it's a discipline that you will carry when your bank account grows from $200, to $500,000.00 . Resist, and I stress the word resist the temptation to spend unnecessary money.

You get a price for a 1(800) phone number, and its only $9.99 a month. You price out a new printer, its only $89.000, business cards only $30.00. Everything seems reasonable, and you can handle the expense.

In retrospect the expenses don't seem much, but this spending creates a habit that will only get worse. Your spending has to be curbed early on, and you need to start making discipline decisions as a businessman/ businesswomen early on.

If your website only made you $8,000.00 in your first year and you spend $2000.00, then you made $6,000 in profit. If you don't manage your spending you could easily spend $4,500 on expenses. Keep your spending down even when your business is making more money.

Apply the same discipline even when your business is making $800,000.00 yearly. In the wrong hands a company making millions can easily be bankrupt. How many times to you see a T.V show showing how the person that won the jackpot in the lottery is now bankrupt.

2 BASICS

Your online business will consist of selling products on the internet. Once set up, you can use your skills to open other websites. For the purpose of this book, I will be showing you how to open a successful reseller website. In the beginning you will be running the entire operation by yourself.

A realistic number that you can try to achieve is $6,000.00 profit in your first year. Yes count the zeros in the number, it's not a misprint. It's not the $1,000,000.00 you were hoping it would be.

Your website will be found by more users the second year. If your running your business correctly, your sales will grow in year two. The trick for year two, is that you take everything you learned from year one and duplicate it.

After running the business for a year you will learn a lot of the niches. You will find what works, and what doesn't. You will take your skills and open another website. Depending on your skills you might start opening a new website every 4 months.

You will also adapt with your market, and might change gears on one of your websites. You will also be constantly working on growing sales on your sites. So in your second year, your first website could be making $20,000.00. Your second, and third website might be making $6,000.00. You decide to open a fourth site that only made you $1,000.00. So in your third year with four sites you can be making $60,000.00 a year. If you grasp the concept and expand to selling on other medias such as Ebay.com and Amazon.com your income can be more.

Of course there will be over achievers that will earn much, much more. There will be people that will make much less. The key thing to remember is that these earning are all made from home. If you get tired of one site, sell it. There are plenty of people that don't know how to start a site, and will pay at least $500.00 for an online store.

As your sales grow, so will your advertising budget. With a bigger budget, your advertising budget can all allow you hire a marketing company. Sales should grow each year.

Your home based business can make you money, but it will not make you rich fast. The risks are very low. You have shopped online before, you might have ordered from a drop shipper without even knowing it.

There are other methods to reselling and making bigger profits. You can buy merchandise directly from China, buy in bulk. This book is only going to focus on drop shipping.

Reseller

You will be a reseller, selling products on the internet to the public for a profit. Your products will be bought from distributors for the purpose of reselling it to a consumer. For the time being you will be dealing with Drop Shipping distributors.

In order to be a reseller you will be dealing with customers. They will have product questions. Your job will be to maintain a relationship, and have customers return.

In order to process the orders you will need a store. This will require you to use software that can handle products, and orders. You will also need a credit card processor to collect the money. All of your customers will be using credit cards, and you will need a processor to handle the charges.

Most processing companies take a few days from the time the customer paid, to the time you see the money available in your account. The fees for the processor very from 2% to 3.9% a transaction. Some have monthly fees, and other don't.

Pay pal has a standard package, with no monthly fees. Currently on low volume sales, they will charge you 2.9%, and .30 cents per transaction.

Distributor

Your distributor buys products from the manufacture. The distributor buys large quantities of products from different manufactures, and warehouses the products. They then sell the products to resellers, and they do not sell to the public. They deal with repeat customers.

Some manufacture don't sell directly to resellers, and you can only buy the product from a distributor. Well established distributors will have stores that buy huge quantities, but they also deal with small stores, and are willing to sell just one.

You will be dealing with drop ship distributors. You're not going to buy products to stock your store. You will be selling products that your drop shipper is stocking.

You will have an account with your drop shipping distributor. Each time you make a sell you will have your drop shipper deliver the product directly to your customer.

They will already have your company name, and logo on file. They will package and ship the item to the customer using your company name, and logo. Your customer will never know that the product came directly from a distributors warehouse. The invoice will have the item without the price, since they don't your selling price. Have you ever received an item and the invoice didn't have the price.

Let examine an example as to how the process works. Let's say you have a website selling Golf Supplies, and you use XYZ as a drop shipper. Your website will be displaying products that you can purchase from XYZ.

You get a customer that visits your store, after he did a search on the net. He searched Fister Golf drivers on Google, and found your store. Your customer purchases a Fister Golf Punisher 450 Driver from your website for $299.00. You just made a sale.

You will log into your distributors website and order the Fister Golf Punisher 450 Driver. Your price is $255.00. You have the item shipped directly to your customer from the distributors warehouse. There is a difference of $45.00 profit minus the $8.97 for using pay pal to process the credit card. You will make $36.03 on an item you didn't have to touch, store, package, or ship.

Customer receives the item, on the shipping box, and invoice he sees your company name. The benefits to this type of arrangement is that you don't have a big overhead. No warehouse, no employees, no rent, and lower risk. Even though your website might have hundreds of products, your entire operation could be running from your bedroom.

Stay Away From Certain Distributors

In business there are many different types of tactic that play on customer. Have you ever caught a furniture store displaying a fake going out of business sales. Then two years later they have the same sale. They are trying to move old merchandise, and want the customer to think he is getting a bargain.

If the furniture store tried the honest approach, Slashing prices on old merchandise to bring in new. Price was originally $600.00, now on sale for $400.00. Some customers might pass this up. They might want the new style merchandise that isn't on sale

Now a dishonest store will play on customers, knowing they enjoy bargains. They instead display going out of business sale, everything must go. They falsely list the couch as originally $800.00 and slash the price to $400.00. The customer feels happier about this purchase. This tactic will sale more couches faster.

Even a street peddler might know how to trick customers. You see a peddler selling the latest I Phone, its brand new in the box. He is asking $80.00 for the phone. You ask him, why is the price so low?. He looks over his shoulder and tells you it fail off the truck, implying its stolen.

You will no longer question the product as authentic, and will feel it's a bargain. Had he told the truth that he bought three dozen phones directly from china, you will examine the phone closer. You will discover the phone is a cheap knock off. This peddlers is selling counterfeit products which is illegal.

He has no store and is untraceable. He will not be there when you return. Stores leave some trail, and will not be selling counterfeit items. When dealing with web stores, they are virtual, and can easily run, and hide.

Sales people know how to manipulate customers. There are different types of approaches. They will squeeze every penny out of you, knowing you will never return.

Distributors are no different. There are honest ones that deal with large resellers for years . There are also ones that know their resellers are going to leave, so they squeeze every penny they can from the ones they get.

When you search for distributor on google.com you will see listings on the top of the page in a shaded box, and some more listings to the right. These are advertisements, you will find some of these companies appear regardless of the type of product you are searching for. They spent a lot of money to be found.

Most of these distributors charge monthly fees, and charge a handling fee to pack your order. They charge fees, so they can pay to secure the top spot on searches. They need to be first because they constantly need new customers.

Consider how easy it was to find these companies. That means thousands of other people found them. Many of these people trying to be resellers have no business skills, which makes them dangerous to you.

You will be competing with thousands of people that also found these distributors. They compete with each other for sales, by lowering their prices. The market is usually flooded.

Resellers will be buying the product for a $10.00 and try to resell it for $10.80. Minus credit card fees, they are making 19 cents profit. Now subtract the monthly fee divided by items sold, and that profit might be just two pennies. Even worse you will have newbies that decides to sell the item for 10.40. Some will spent heavily on advertising, and at the end of the month they are losing money. However their sloppy business, will be costing you money.

These drop shippers charge a monthly fee, to ensures that even if you never make a sale, they still profit. The item that they sell for $10.00 they are making $2.50 in mark up, and a few more bucks by overcharging on the shipping and handling.

These companies are legit, they are not using bad tactics. They just know that they need to profit from their new customer, and also know that the majority will not be repeat customers. They dabble the line of distributor and reseller

Some drop shippers will even have a relationship with a web design company to make you an automated website. They make the process easy. The company will charge you a monthly fee for hosting, running, and maintaining the site. Some will even handle the sales. So for $20.00 a month, and some have the nerve to take a percentage of your sales, you will have a website that you don't have to do a single thing for. So why do they need you?

The question you should ask yourself, is if it's that easy, why doesn't the distributor set up this automated website with a 30% mark up above their existing mark up.

This type of set up, monthly fee to the distributor, monthly fee to have an automated website, attracts the people that rather take diet pills instead of exercising. Even worse I have seen them advertise that you can make $100,000.00 in your first year. This is how your business brain should question this things. So you and the three hundred other people that just bought the same website, and are selling the same products are all making $100,000.00. You are the latter, and will not fall for this type of set up.

A good distributor makes their money from the profit on the sales, and has been around for a long time. His clients stores are making money. Resellers are constantly seeking customers. Unlike resellers, distributors have the same repeat customers for years.

Another thing to be weary of is the fake distributors, or wholesalers that are really resellers. Find out if they have a warehouse, ask questions about the size. If they tell you that they ship directly from the manufacture, then they are misrepresenting themselves.

This is a dirty sales tactic. They advertise as wholesalers, to make people believe they are getting bargains. They attract people looking for bargains, and for someone that is looking for a whole seller.

Some distributors require that you open an account before they show you the price on items. This is a practice that protects the resellers. The public will not be able to know your prices.

If they require that you have to join to see their prices, ask them if they can give you their wholesale price on three items. Explain to the them you want to research the market before you commit. Google the product and compare their price to other resellers on the internet.

3 GETTING STARTED

This is the hardest step, to overcome. Read the entire chapter before committing to any of the steps. This will ensure that you don't jump into anything without fully understanding.

There are hundreds of hosting companies, and options. You can research and use any product that you like. I will be recommending companies to help the novice, and give you a starting point.

Conducting your own research can yield better results. If you found a webhosting company that is better, then there is no reason not to use it. I will also be asking you to conduct your own research in certain things. Each State rules are different. It's best if you did your research and get up to date information.

To start your store you have to find a product that you want to sell. You will need to buy a domain name, and web hosting. You will have to register your business, and file for a reseller certificate. Then you will need a secure server.

Here are the steps in order:
1. Find products
2. Buy You Domain, Webhosting, and Secure Server
3. Find a shopping cart
4. Set Up Your Entity
   Create Your Sole Proprietorship
   Get a reseller certificate
5. Personalize Your website, and set up your products
6. Apply and get a credit card processor

All the steps will be explained and clarified. The cost will vary depending on your choices. Webhosting and domain name will run you about $50 dollars for the first year with siteground.com. They charge more for the second year. To file a Sole Proprietorship will average about $150. Secure website will cost about $80.00 yearly. A shopping cart will vary from free to $800.00. A credit card processor will range from free to about $30.00 a month plus a percentage of your sales.

FINDING PRODUCTS

You need to decide the type of products you want to start selling. If you can't think of something, start thinking about your hobbies. It's easier to start with something you love, and know about. If you don't have a hobby then get one, people with hobbies live longer.

Let's explore the type of things that might interest you. Do you like to fish, skateboard, or go camping. Do you love to golf, or work out? In high school did you enjoy playing soccer. How about building models, or making your own skateboards. Do you love collecting clocks, baseball cards, or hats.

Can't think of a hobby, then start thinking about what you like. Is it your cat, your child, baking. I am about to give you a few websites that you can explore, and perhaps you can come up with an idea.

Please remember I have never used or endorse the companies below.

https://dropshipdirect.com
https://www.dandh.com
http://www.wynit.com
http://www.petra.com
http://www.moteng.com

While checking out the websites you notice they all have something in common. They do not sell their products to the public, and they do not charge a monthly fee. If you decide to use one of these websites your search is over.

I would stay away from adult clothes, shoes and jewelry. They tend to have a higher return rate, and customers always have questions. Baby clothing tend to have a lower rate than adult lines.

Let's say you want to sell pet supplies, try searching pet supply drop shipper. You will be over whelmed with pages. Take your time and go through at least 12 pages. You will start to see certain traps, that some companies have set up.

Now that you searched Pet supply drop shipper, type Pet supply distributor. You will see different companies. Search a least 12 pages clicking on sites that interest you. Once you found a company that you like, do some research. If it's a distributor, and on their website they don't mention drop shipping give them a call. Ask them if they are willing to drop ship.

Now review their shipping policy, and return policy. Make sure it's clearly written. If the company appears to your liking, now Google for complaints against the company.

Contact the company, and explain to them you are new to the business, and ask for assistance. Ask if they can help you with the product uploads to your website, and for advice. If you feel the love from the company, then it might be time to commit.

This is going to be a long lasting marriage with the company. Divorce always costs money. You want to find one company, and use the company exclusively. Having two companies may seem as a good idea, but could create problems.

Suppose a customer orders two products, one is sold by one drop shipper located in New Jersey, and the other in Ohio. You will be paying separate shipping, two different tracking numbers, and two different arrivals. Now suppose your customer wants to return both items. The mixing of two companies in one store isn't a good idea.

Setting up Your Website

Now let's say you have found your drop shipper, it's time to create your company. Find a web hosting company, to start your website. If you don't have one use www.siteground.com. In the search box, type domain name, click on the link. Start. searching for a domain name that is available.

Keep the name as simple as possible. However this is easier said than done. A single word name would be the best name. However finding one will be a challenge. Big companies have paid good money to buy single name domain names. Type in pets.com, and you're redirected to mypetsmart.com

In reality you will find a domain name using two words, or three words. Avoid using more than 4 words in the domain. GoergeandKellybestpetssupplies.com is too long. Sorry George, but perhaps Kellyspetsupply.com would be a better choice. At the time of print the name was available, so I am not endorsing it. You want people to remember your name, and for it to be catchy.

Now that you found an available name, purchase the name. To set up the hosting pay for a year, or for at least six months. Remember your hosting, and domain name are two separate things. You can pay for a domain name, without purchasing hosting. So if you are already thinking about your next store, purchase the domain name to protect it from being sold.

Shopping Cart

It's time to set up a shopping cart. Search for shopping carts, and you will find over a dozen good ones. You don't want to be committed to one that requires a monthly fee, or a percentage of your sales.

The shopping cart will be the software that will allow you to operate the store. It will have the ability to do mass uploads of products. The cart will be the interphase that will allow customers to create accounts, and place orders. It will connect the purchaser with your credit card processor. You want the cart to be user friendly.

While your shopping for a cart, there are key features to look for. It should allow for easy uploading products to Google Merchant. It should allow you to create a sitemap. The cart should allow for returns. You may want it to seamlessly allow customers to use their Facebook account to log into your store.

If your using siteground.com they have a list of carts that they can install for you. Zen cart is free, CS-Cart is free for a trail version, and then you have to purchase the license. Ask your drop shipper if they have a shopping cart that they like. It will be easier to integrate, and maintain the inventory.

The shopping cart will be the feel of the store. The cart you choose will display the products. It will email you when there is an order. It will allow customers to log in, and check their orders. If you don't know which cart then use CS-Cart try the free version before you commit.

Now that you have your domain name, and website write something on your page. Type in on the homepage, welcome to my pet supply store insert name, You will find many great pet supplies, we will be open for business soon! Repeat in the homepage that you sell pet supplies.

Your new website has no Google rating, it still doesn't exist. You want your page up and running, even though you're not ready to open it. You want the internet to learn that you exist.

Set up the top header of your page to reflect your company name. It could say something like welcome to myname.com, or something simple with your websites name in it. Currently it will be saying the shopping carts name.

Each cart will be different to change, and you might have to Google, how do I change the page title in Cs-Cart, or Zen-cart or whichever cart you selected. I will walk you through the process if you set up your store with CS-Cart. Type in your websitename.com/admincp.php, and log in.

Click on design in the upper right of screen. Click on blocks, and when the page load click on all pages. You will see page title, erase the current title and type yours in. Then add a meta description; Low prices on all pet supplies. Below you will see Key words, add about 8 good keywords, such as Dog beds, cat supplies, pet supplies, etc.

Now when Google crawls your page it will understand that your site is about selling pet supplies. Your giving your website a chance to mature. Currently if you search for site, you will not find it.

Create Your Entity

The tax laws have changed, and your credit card processor is mandated in reporting your earnings. You also need a reseller certificate for most distributors to do business with you. So in keeping with the law you have to set up your entity.

There are different types you can set up, Corporations, LLC, and Sole Proprietorship. Sole proprietor has the least protection of the three. However for your first website this is probably the easiest. As a sole proprietorship you will have no employees, and you will have a simpler tax return. When the time comes when you grow to multiple websites you can always create a LLC cooperation.

If you're going to use your name as the business you might not be required to file a sole proprietorship in your State. If you are going to include what your business is, then you're going to have to. If you state what you do, then it's considered a DBA.

If I start a business named George Astras then I might not be required to register in certain States. If I start a business called George's Marine Paints, or Discount Marine Paint, then I am Doing

17

Business AS, Marine Paint, and will be required to file for a Sole Proprietor

Since each state is different, you would have to Google, How to start a sole proprietorship in your state. In NYC it costs about $120.00, you have to file a business certificate in your local county Clerk's office. A driver license, notarizing, and your sole proprietorship is set up the same day.

After you set up your sole proprietor, use Google, and search how to obtain a resell certificate in your state. As a sole proprietor you do not need an EIN number with the IRS. You can use your social security number. If you want an EIN number visit the IRS website, and apply for it online.

With the exception of a few States, you're going to be required to collect sales tax for items sold to people in your state. If the item is exempt in your State from Sales tax then you don't have to collect sales tax.

If you base your business in NY, and get an order from someone in NY, you will have to collect Sales Tax on the order. If you get an order from someone in Maine you will not be required to collect sales tax. You will be required to pay the sales tax quarterly to your State. Some items are exempt, In NY if you sell a US Flags or NY State flag then you don't have to collect sale taxes on those items. Do not get confused, this tax is different from your obligation to pay taxes on your earnings.

Currently there is a 1992 Supreme Court ruling the stated that States cannot require mail-order businesses to collect sales tax unless they have a physical presence in that State. However the laws are constantly changing, and there is currently legislation on the topic.

The topic is Dawning, and requires a more update view by you at the time of your opening. I found Nolo's website informative, and I often refer it to it for guide. Here is a link: http://www.nolo.com/legal-encyclopedia/50-state-guide-internet-sales-tax-laws.html

Now that you have created your entity go and apply for a checking account. Bring your sole proprietorship paper work, reseller certificate, driver license or other proof of address that matches the address on the business. Open the account in the entities name. You will use this account for your credit card processor, and for your business.

You next step will be to obtain a company to process your credit cards. Most credit card processing companies want to see an actual store before they accept you. Therefore we will now have to set up your website.

Contact the drop shipper that you found, and open the account with them. They will now give you access to their products. Most will have files that you can mass upload to your shopping cart.

Personalize Your Website

Start setting up categories and make your products easy to find. Take a peek at your competitors site. Make a logo on the page. You want to have an identity. It can be something as simple as having the word Pet Store in blue letters, with the E in Yellow. If you have an artsy side to you, then express it by drawing your logo.

It will give your store an identity. The majority of drop shippers can include it on the invoice. My two year old hasn't learned to read but can identify stores based on their logos. She can easily identify any McDonalds, but is unable to identify other fast food chains. She can spot a Toy R Us better than anyone I know.

It's time to set up your email account. You will log into your websites c-panel. There you will find an email account set up. Create an email, such as orders@yourdomainname.com. Set this email as your default in your cart. Set up this email to forward to an email account that you always check.

If you have an android phone have the email forwarded to the account on your phone, so you can stay on top of the emails. Sprint has two companies Virgin, and Boost that offer unlimited talk, and web for a set monthly fee.

Your drop shipper will have product files that you can download. They will make loading all their products to your site fast. However remember that the file will have the whole sale price. Make sure you do a global update and have the price displayed on your site include your profit margin.

Learn the process of mass file up load, and then learn how to upload just the product id, and stock number. If time permits you will be updating the inventory of your store to correspond your drop suppliers inventory daily. This will take you about five minutes and will minimize receiving orders that your supplier has sold out. If you can't update the inventory daily, try to do it at least twice weekly.

You're going to have to set up a contact page. Provide a link, where a customer can email you. Provide a phone number. If you can't answer calls remove the number after you get your contract with your credit card processor. The credit card processor requires you to have a store, with a contact number, shipping policy, privacy policy and a return policy.

You're going to have to create pages stating your shipping, and return policy. You can have your customers return the product directly to your distributor. Pass your distributors restocking fees to your customer plus another 3% to offset the credit card fees. So if your distributor charges you a 5% restocking fee, state in your policy that your restocking fee is 8%.

If your distributor allows you thirty days to return a product, your policy should be shorter, let's say 20 days. Make it clear that they require an RMA before returning the item. You will be required an RMA from your distributor.

If you have the money to pay for the products before the money settles, then you can offer same day shipping. If you have to wait for the money, then state in your policy it takes 2-3 days to process the order.

You will get customers that are antsy, and will contact their credit card company if they don't have a tracking number right away. It is important that you have your shipping policy displayed. When you get the tracking number make sure you email your customers they will appreciate the communication.

Some distributors charge a flat rate on shipping, others charge depending on the current rates of the shipper. Whichever the case charge your customers 10% more on shipping than what you're paying. If it cost you $20.00 for shipping, charge your customers $22.00.

Take this extra 10 percent and put it aside. You will encounter fraudulent orders, and this extra 10 percent will help you off set it. Consider this as a self-insurance. In your policy state that you can only ship to the billing address.

I will explain this in detail later, but for your first three years you should not ship outside the United States, and do not ship to a different address other than the billing address. Make this a strict policy.

Here is an example for your shipping page:

Please allow 2-3 days for orders to process. We use Fed-Ex, and UPS to ship merchandise. We will email you the tracking number when your order ships. Currently we are unable to process international orders. We only ship to the Billing Address.

Here is an example for your return page:

All items purchased can be returned within 10 business days from the date the order is complete. Orders are not considered complete until the item is delivered. Returned products must be complete in the original packaging and resalable. Special Order items may not be returned. Units requiring service, either warranty or otherwise, should be returned directly to the appropriate manufacturer. Shipping and handling will not be returned, and you are responsible for the shipping and handling back. A 3% stocking fee will be charged on all returns. An approval number is required prior to you returning the merchandise. If you have any questions, feel free to email us at orders@yourdomainname.com.

Credit Card Processors

Now that you have your store set up with products, contact your credit card processor to set up an account. You have two major choices in the market. You can use Pay pal, or Authorize.net.

Authorize.net will require that you use a merchant to accept the payment. They have a list of merchant on their website. Each merchant charges different amounts to allow you to process credit cards. If you can't decide try Transfirst.

Your website is required to have certain pages for the credit processer company to approve your account. The shipping and return policy should be clearly stated, You can copy and paste your suppliers pages, and edit them to fit your store.

It will take a few days for the money to show up in your account after a purchase. If you are going to wait for the funds to clear, then it's necessary to state in your shipping policy orders take1-3 days to process.

The cart will have an area where you can enter your authorize.net or paypal.com account numbers to allow it to process the credit cards. Set your security setting with the processor that the entire billing address has to match for approval. Set up your shopping cart that it only allows shipping to the billing address.

The credit card processor will keep a percentage of the total transaction amount. They also add a flat rate fee for each transaction. They might be charging you 2.00% and .30 cents for each transaction. The fee is taken from the total which includes the shipping. For example you sell a dog house for $80.00, and the shipping is $20.00. The total order amount is $100. The credit card processor will keep $2.30 for processing the order.

If you want to accept America Express you will have to ask your processor to add them. The payment schedule will be different for American Express.

The credit card processor will automatically deposit the funds into your account. However they also have the ability to withdraw money from your account. It is a wise idea to have a separate account for your business. You don't want your personal account drained. You can read more about this in the next chapter.

MAKING A PROFIT

You have to decide on a profit margin. You will find that other stores might be selling with just a 5% mark up. The profit margin is your decision. It might be tempting to make your margin small to compete. I rather have one order with a 15% margin then two orders with a 5% margin. You have credit card fees, hosting fees, and be working completing more orders for less. At 5% you can't offer incentives, and try different marketing strategies.

A comfortable margin can be at 15%. You will be cheaper than most brick and mortar stores. You will also have room to run gimmicks, or sales. You can track the success of your marketing by offering sales.

Let's say you sale golf supplies. You might want to contact resorts in Myrtle Beach, and ask them if they can hang up your flyer. Explain to them that you will offer their guests 10% off for being a hotel guest. Create a coupon code with the resorts name in it. So if your offering Hilton customers 10%, then the customer will have to enter Hilton in the coupon box on your site.

The hotel is rewarding their customers, and you are getting referrals. If you see sales using Hilton in the promotional box, then you know that the marketing is working. Your customers feel that they got a bargain. Best of all you got visitors.

You might want to offer customers that bought from you a sale in the future. You can reward customers that purchased something from you. Let's say a year after they bought something you send them an email, with a 10% coupon.

I want to plant some ideas while you dabble over the margin. The profit margin is your decision, and can be changed to compete. You can have different margins for each products. If your selling laptops, you can have the computers priced at a 10% margin. Since most customers will research the price of the laptop. Once they find your price cheaper, they will buy the laptop. They might also buy a mouse, which your margin is 20%.

4 THE SCAMMERS

The world wide world has many advantages for everybody. It also provides the opportunity for criminals to operate with ease. If you own a brick and mortar store you are at risk that an armed robber could walk in and steal what you have worked hard for. The same can happen on the internet.

On the web however the chance of getting robbed is much higher, and you have to protect yourself. Depending on the type of products you sell, you will be targeted more often. If you cell GPS units they are coming at you more than if you sell baby hats.

The sad truth is that no one cares. Your fraudulent order is too small for Federal Law Enforcement to investigate. Since it was shipped outside your city, or State, it will also be out of the jurisdiction of your local police.

You have to aware of the criminal element, to protect yourself. You want to spot suspicious orders. You get an order for $12.00 from John Doe, and ten minutes later, the same person places a second order. Do they love your store so they came back?

The credit card processor you are using will have safe guards. Set the setting that the credit card number and billing address have to match. That means that when they enter the stolen credit card number they have to enter the correct billing address to get the charge approved. The general setting is usually to have the zip code match. Also require the CSV code.

This might cause you to lose some customers. They will not be able to use gift cards, or temporary cards. People that have moved, or people that want   the merchandise shipped to their work place. However depending in the type of merchandise you sell, it isn't worth the thousands that you can lose.

Without this feature set up the criminal can use a fake billing address, and have the item shipped to this fake address. You won't have the opportunity to red flag the order, since you are unable to see that the billing address they entered isn't the actual billing address.

With this safe guard in place the criminal is forced to enter the correct billing address. They will have to enter a separate shipping address, so they can receive it.. They will usually have the items shipped to an address in the same State as the victim's to reduce suspicion.

Once the victim discovers that their identity was stolen, they file a claim with their credit card company. The credit card company reverses the charges, and the money is automatically taken out from your account.

You have to provide proof with a tracking number, and signature that the item was received. If the shipping address is different from the real billing address you will lose the money. The credit card company will hold you responsible, and you will be out the money.

To avoid this from happening you can set up your shopping cart to only allow shipping to the billing address. The customer will not have the option to ship to a different address.

Without this safe guard in place you might get ten fraudulent, all shipped to different addresses before you catch on. Once the criminal finds a store he can order from, they will continue to place orders, until the store shuts them out.

There are many different scams to obtain credit card numbers, so the amount of fraud on the net is frightening. You have to protect yourself. If you shipped the item to the billing address, you have a fighting chance to recover your money.

One popular scam that seems to target electronics is run by people in Russia. The credit card numbers and identity are gathered by various means. They can even buy them on the internet.. There are websites that allow buyers, and sellers of identity theft to meet.

They can get them from a sales clerk that has access to credit cards. The person selling airline tickets has to check Id, and is able to get the billing address. The credit card usually has enough money or credit since the person is expecting travel expenses.

The scammer will then post ads on craiglist.org for work at home jobs. The person answering the ad, is given a fake job. They are told they will be shippers for whatever reason. They might be told that merchandise will be shipped to their home to avoid international taxes, or that websites do not ship to Russia.

They are told that they will receive packages, and then print a prepaid label, reship the package to Russia. They are told they will be paid by the package. One person was told five dollars a package, and by then end of the month they thought they earned $10,000.00.

The majority of the people reshipping packages are never paid, or are told they can keep one of the orders. The scammer using stolen credit card numbers buy merchandise, and have the item shipped to this person address. They are sending a couple of hundred packages to this persons house. They email them prepaid shipping labels, and have the packages send to Russia.

The person who answered the ad is held holding criminal charges if any. The scam continues with new people answering the ad. The scammers have a good sense of which sites to target. They are doing this scam hundreds of times a month.

They create an email for the order and it's usually a variation of the victims name @gmail.com or yahoo.com. They provide fake phone numbers if the website requires a phone number. They use IP software to mask their location.

They can hit a website numerous times without them knowing. They have stolen cards in numerous States, and have people set up to receive them in each. So by the time a site realizes that they were hit, sometimes a few months after the orders, they have been taken for several thousands of dollars.

If you only ship merchandize to the billing address the scammer can't receive the item, and will move on to an easier site. This doesn't stop other local criminals from trying. If someone orders two or more of the same expensive item, contact the buyer. If your gut still tells you there something wrong request that the shipping requires a signature, or cancel the order. If the order turns out fraudulent, you can provide proof that you shipped it to the billing address, and a signature was acquired.

Around the Christmas holiday your site might experience a surge in sales, watch them and don't stray from shipping to a different address other than the billing. Come January there is going to be customers that can't pay their credit card bill. They will claim fraudulent charges, to avoid paying. Since you are not Santa Clause you don't want to pay for their gifts. Be ready to provide tracking numbers.

Then there are simple scammers, they usually involve someone that has access to credit cards, and tries to use them . It can be a waiter or waitress, or a skimmer at the ATM machine. Since these people don't know the billing address, they can't get past having the order approved on your site. They will move to another site.

How about the person that works at the ticket line at the airport. They have the credit card number, and the owners address from the Id they had to provide. Hotel clerks have the same access. The ability to steal credit card numbers is limitless. You have to be aware of these criminals to avoid accepting fraudulent orders.

Watch for orders that were declined because they tried the wrong billing address. Then placed another successful order shipping to the billing address however upgraded the shipping to overnight. Your laughing because it's obvious, but it's only obvious if you are aware of scammers. Cancel this order, and refund the money.

If you see a declined order because the purchase exceeded the credit card limits, and then they tried again and got approved for something cheaper. Cancel the order, refund the money, and email them saying it failed your Fraud Protection.

Sometimes the scammer is easy to spot just as long as you know where to look. Check the IP address of the orders for the day, and for the week. If you see one repeating, but different people made orders, cancel all the orders, and refund the money.

If you see a completed order for a small amount, and then shortly after a second order for a large amount by the same person be weary. They tested the card to see if they can make an order, and then went in for the big amount.

You should restrict shipping orders outside the United States. You are not ready for the scammers outside the US. You are offered very little protection for shipping outside the States.

When your site is making a ton of money then you can loosen some of the restrictions. You will be able to afford a few thousand dollars in fraudulent charges a year. Until then do not flex or ease up on these strict shipping policies.

The scammers are always evolving, and will try new tactics. Don not let them intimidate you, if your careful you can make it through the year without any fraud.

5 MARKETING

You want your site to be found as soon as possible. The more sites that have your website listed the better your ranking will be. Search engines send out Web Crawlers to websites and scan the page content. This allows them to know the content on websites. If an established site has your domain listed, then the Web Crawlers will visit you website.

Your first step is to visit addme.com and enter your website. Then do the same with dmoz.org. Visit Manta and create an account. You want your website to appear in as many possible locations as possible. The internet gives you a chance for thousands to find you.

Since you are newly established you might want to learn from companies that have been successful. Visit Alexa.com and search your competitors, and see how many link ins they have. You are going to have to create an account, to view all the link ins.

I will try to simplify this long process. Google will rank your website based on popularity. You want a high rank so your website can be found on the first page of searches. Who cares if you're the cheapest, if your website shows up on page twenty on searches. Your customers will never find you.

The best way to improve your rank is to have link ins. That means other websites have links to your website. Look at Alexa.com search a few companies in your field. Your completion might have 2,000 link ins. Your job is to have a link to your site from at least 20 of their linked in sites.

You want to get to 2,000 links, but it will take time. There are companies that will charge and give you a thousand link ins. However the links aren't natural, and Google can penalize you, giving you a bad rating.

Now let us stay with the pet supply theme, type a search for pet beds blog, or bird cages blog, dog grooming blog. Join the blogs and answer or type as many articles as you can. Create a link to one of your product pages. You are creating links to your website.

On your webpage create informational articles. The search engines will find them and send people your way. Write an article on the best practices in grooming your dog, or how to properly use the electric collar. This will send people that search How to groom my dog, to your page. Find blogs on the topic, and join the blog. Tell people you found an article about the topic, and send them to your webpage. Never get tired of adding places that people will find you.

With a simple camera you can make a short video showing you using the electric collar, upload the video to You tube, and create a link to your site.

 Improve your website by adding key words. In each category page write a small description. This will help the web crawler understand your page. On the category page for Dog dishes, you can write; You will find many dog dishes in this section. We have all types of dog dishes. We have large and small dog dishes, and self-feeding dishes.

Each product page and category will have a box for key words, add key words to all your categories. Explain the products, and try to use 8 or less key words. You can be general in your key words. On your home page you can type pet supplies, pet products, pet beds etc. In your category page type the products found in that section.

The next place to add your website, will be Google Merchant. You will upload your products to Google. The product will be displayed with the price when someone searches for it.

You can also pay for advertising to have your site found. There are sites such as shopping.com which has now joined forces with Bing, that charge you a fee for each customer they send you. Google has Adwords that charge you for each click on keywords that you have selected. If you create such an account try not to be general. You will lose a lot of advertising money.

If you pay 2.00 for the keyword Pet supplies, you will get a lot of hits. You can easily spent $400.00 a day in hits, and spend more than your profit. Make a keyword more specific to items you have. Such as Durapet dog bowl, let's say for 30 cents for each click they send you. You might only get two click a day for that search term, but will have a greater sale/profit ratio.

The person typing the search word pet supplies might be searching for dog ice scream or a local pet store. They click on your ad, and quickly leave your store, you were not what they were searching for. This click cost you $2.00.

More specific key words will be cheaper to bid on. Durapet dog dish would be cheaper to bid on, and your ad will be on the first page of searches. The price of key words depends on what others are paying for the key word.

If the top price is 60 cents, then the person paying 60 cents per click will be first in searches. If you want to be first then you will have to bid higher than 60 cents per click. Remember your paying for each click, regardless if the person makes a purchase.

So a keyword such as Durapet dog dishes will be cheaper than a general key word such as pet supplies. If you bid about 30 cents, you will not be first on the page, but will be on the first page.

If they type Durapet dog bowl have an ad that states about dog bowls, and links to your dog bowls section. You will lose customers if they click on your ad, and they land on you homepage. The budget is up to you, but until your making big sales, I would put a limit of $4.00 a day.

Create a Facebook account for your website, have your friends join the page, and have it active. Upload stories, and pictures. Create a Facebook link on your website so customers can join your page. Facebook is a great marketing tool

More often people forget the personal touch to promoting. Successful real estate agents are always promoting themselves. At a wedding or any other social event the majority of the people at the event will know the real estate agent. The agent would of made their way around and gotten to know as many people as possible. They are good and natural and what they do, which is self-promotion.

You will now be acting as a successful professional agent. When your pet visits the vet, strike up casual conversions with others in the waiting room. Ask them their pets name, how old, and before the conversion is over let them know you just opened up a pet store. Let the vet know that you started one, and ask him if he can help you. Offer his customers a discount. Your shopping cart should have a feature where you can create promo words for discounts.

Create a photo contest, where the top three winners gets credit to your store. Print flyers for your store, and always have them with you. At the dog park engage people in conversation, and give them a flyer. If you see them entering the contest, send them an email thanking them, adding that personal touch. When a customer buys something, send them an email about the contest. Your quest to create customers and repeat customers has begun.

This can be done with any type of store, create a fishing contest, or anything else you can imagine. While shopping if you see someone interested in something you sell give them a flyer. Always have flyers with a 5% discount promo code.

Old fashioned but it still works, contact professionals in your field that don't sale your products. Contact at least 50 vets each month, announcing your store. Tell them about your store, and if they can help promote it. Offer their customers a discount. Don't insult them by offering a percentage of the sale. With the web you can easily find their email address. Make the greeting personal, and the body generic. For example:

Hello Dr. Moss,

I am an enthusiastic pet owner, and have recently started an online store mydomain.com. As a professional in the field I want to offer you a 10% discount on all of your orders. I would also appreciate any business your office can send my way. I can mail you a flyer with a promo code that will allow your customers to enjoy a 5% discount on their orders. If you enjoy my website, email me back, and I will send you your 10% promo code, and separate promo code for your customers. I will follow up by sending you the flyer be email or mail depending on your preference. Thank you for time, and serving pets.

This can be done for any type of business that you started, wedding favors-contact wedding halls, selling sex toys then put on the dark glasses and visit adult video stores. If you sell children's toys, it might be illegal to post flyers in the park, so you have to get creative.

Buy buckets at the 99 cent store, and use a paint marker and write on it. Donate the buckets to the sand box. Parents will see the buckets that will have Donated by yourdomain.com written on it. Ask gyms that have a day care if you can post a flyer in the day care.

Marketing is where you will excel and increase your sales. You have to work hard, and there is no magic pill. Earlier you read that your first year profit can only be $6,000.00, and you continued to read the book. There is a driving force inside you that says that is too little, and you will strive to make more. That is the winning attitude, that will make you succeed.

www.ingramcontent.com/pod-product-compliance
Lightning Source LLC
Chambersburg PA
CBHW071548170526
45166CB00004B/1586